How To Increase
Millions Of Jobs
In A Year

USA can increase 45.7 million jobs in a year if economic policy described in this book is adopted.

If job of undocumented people is stopped, 8 million jobs will be increased and Government revenue will increase $36.4 Billion dollars in a year. In addition, Billions dollars Govt expense to control undocumented people could be reduced.

$914 Billion dollar purchasing power of USA people could be increased in a year and no business or company will close down for lack of sale. In addition, Billions dollars Govt revenue will increase from sale tax and income tax.

USA Government revenue will increase $208 Billion dollars in a year.

Present economic recession was created by wrong economic policy of the USA Government. Economic recession will be over within a few months, permanently and will never come back if policy described in this book is adopted.

This book can help to other countries to increase job and Government revenue.

How To Increase Millions Of Jobs In A Year

Abdus Shahid

To order additional copies of this book, contact:
Xlibris Corporation
1-888-795-4274
www.Xlibris.com
Orders@Xlibris.com
92514

CONTENTS

TABLES

CHARTS

ABDUS SHAHID (M.S.DOUBLE, ECONOMICS)

Author has 18 years economic research experience in 3
different countries including 5 years in USA.

PREFACE

I wrote this important research oriented book based on economic crisis of United States of America. This book will help to other countries also to increase employment and Government revenue. Millions of people of USA are jobless. Billions of dollars deficit budget for the country, states and the cities. In addition thousands of business closed for lack of income. In addition, government had to spend Billions dollars for food stamp and welfare.

Government tax revenue decreased seriously. Purchasing power of the people has decreased seriously. Government has given lump sum money to increase purchasing power. But, it does not increase purchasing power and it does not stop closing of business. Government made about one trillion dollar stimulus plan to increase jobs. But, it could not create job for all jobless people. New Graduates are coming from colleges but they have no jobs. Government is spending Billions Dollars for unemployment insurance. Government is spending Billions Dollars subsidies for shelter of jobless people.

This research oriented book will find out the cause of serious unemployment in USA. How millions of jobs can be increased within a year. How Billions Dollars Government revenue can be increased within a year. How the economic recession has been created? How economic recession can be removed. How Billions Dollars purchasing power of the people can be increased.

This book is equally applicable for other countries of the world who are suffering about same type of economic problems like USA.

CHAPTER 1:

CAUSES OF SERIOUS UNEMPLOYMENT IN USA

1.1. USA transferred 21.8 million jobs to other countries in 2000 and 45.7 million jobs in 2008:

USA cannot increase millions of jobs for it's people transferring 45.7 million jobs to other countries in 2008. USA transferred 21.8 million jobs to other countries in 2000. USA economy was much better at that time. USA Job transfer to other countries increased almost every year after that. In 2008 USA transferred 45.7 million jobs to other countries (Table: 1).

Table 1.Total number of jobs USA transferred to other countries from 2000-2008 (in millions)									
	2000	**2001**	**2002**	**2003**	**2004**	**2005**	**2006**	**2007**	**2008**
Total job transferred from USA(in Millions)	21.8	20.6	23.4	26.6	32.8	38.6	41.4	40.5	45.7
Increase of job transfer each year(in Millions)	Base*	-1.2	2.8	3.2	6.2	5.9	2.8	-0.9	5.3

Increase of job transfer	Base*	-1.2	1.6	4.8	11.0	16.8	19.6	18.7	23.9
from 2000(in Millions)									
*Keeping 2000 as base year.									

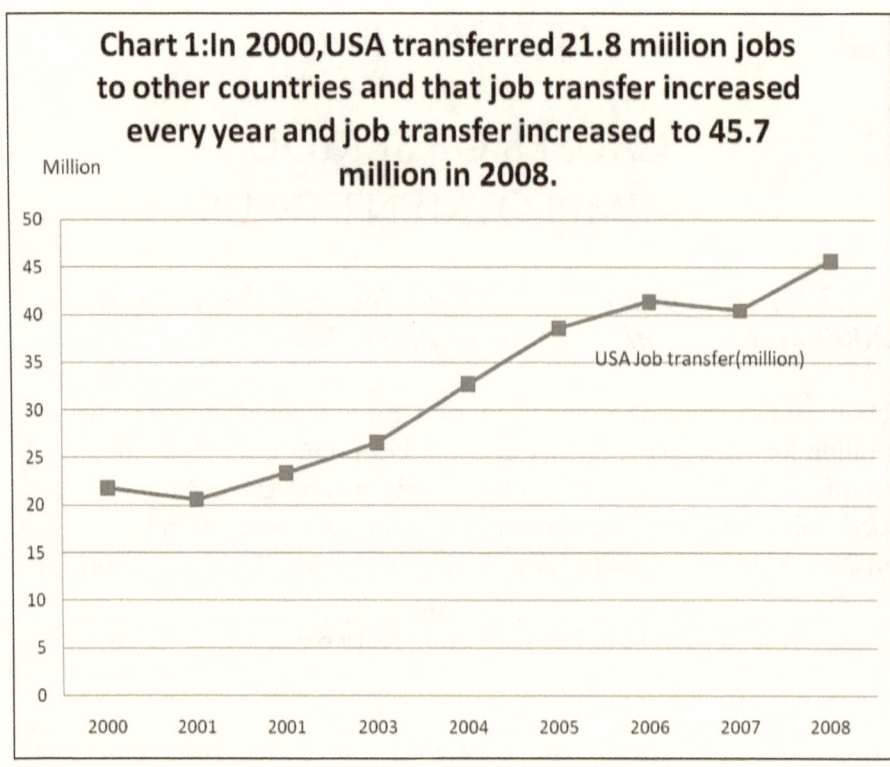

Chart 1:In 2000,USA transferred 21.8 miilion jobs to other countries and that job transfer increased every year and job transfer increased to 45.7 million in 2008.

So, USA job transfer increased 23.9 million from 2000 to 2008. USA economy became worse in 2008. This indicates the negative correlation between job transfer and strength of economy. If USA job transfer to other countries increases, USA economy goes down and vice versa.

1.2. Total USA job transfer to other countries were 21.8 million in 2000; 20.6 million in 2001; 23.4 million in 2002; 26.6 million in 2003; 32.8 million in 2004; 38.6 million in 2005; 41.4 million in 2006; 40.5 million in 2007; 45.7 million in 2008:

Total USA job transfer to other countries were 21.8 million in 2000; 20.6 million in 2001; 23.4 million in 2002; 26.6 million in 2003; 32.8 million in 2004; 38.6 million in 2005; 41.4 million in 2006; 40.5 million in 2007; 45.7 million in 2008(Table:1). USA job transfer increased 18.7 million in 2007 than 2000. USA job transfer increased 19.6 million in 2006 than 2000. USA job transfer increased 16.8 million in 2005 than 2000. 2.8 million more jobs were transferred in 2003 than 2002. Similarly, 3.2 million more jobs were transferred in 2004 than 2003. Again, 5.3 million more jobs were transferred in 2008 than 2007. So, USA economy is going toward worse every year due to increased transfer of jobs every year.

1.3. USA has serious trade deficit with other countries. In 2000 USA had $436 Billion Dollars trade deficit with other countries. In 2008 USA had $914 Billion Dollars trade deficit with other countries:

USA trade deficit were $412 Billon dollar in 2001, $468 Billion dollar in 2002, $532 Billion dollar in 2003, $655 Billion dollar in 2004, $772 Billion dollar in 2005, $828 Billion dollar in 2006, $809 Billion dollar in 2007, $914 Billion dollar in 2008(Table: 2). It has been proved that there is negative correlation between trade deficit and strength of the Economy/ job. If trade deficit increases, job goes down and economy goes down and vice versa. So, trade deficit must be reduced to zero or close to zero to increase job and to increase strength of economy. So, import from other countries must be reduced to export level to that country to increase job in USA. If a country has unemployment problem, the country should not import those merchandise from other countries which the people of the country can make.

Table 2. Total merchandise export and import from 2000-2008 (in Billion dollar).

		2000	2001	2002	2003	2004	2005	2006	2007	2008
Total($ Billion)	Export	782	729	693	725	815	901	1,026	1,148	1,287
Total($ Billion)	Import	1,218	1,141	1,161	1,257	1,470	1,673	1,854	1,957	2,201
Total($Billion)	Trade Balance (Negative)	(436)	(412)	(468)	(532)	(655)	(772)	(828)	(809)	(914)
Source: US Statistical Abstract, 2009										

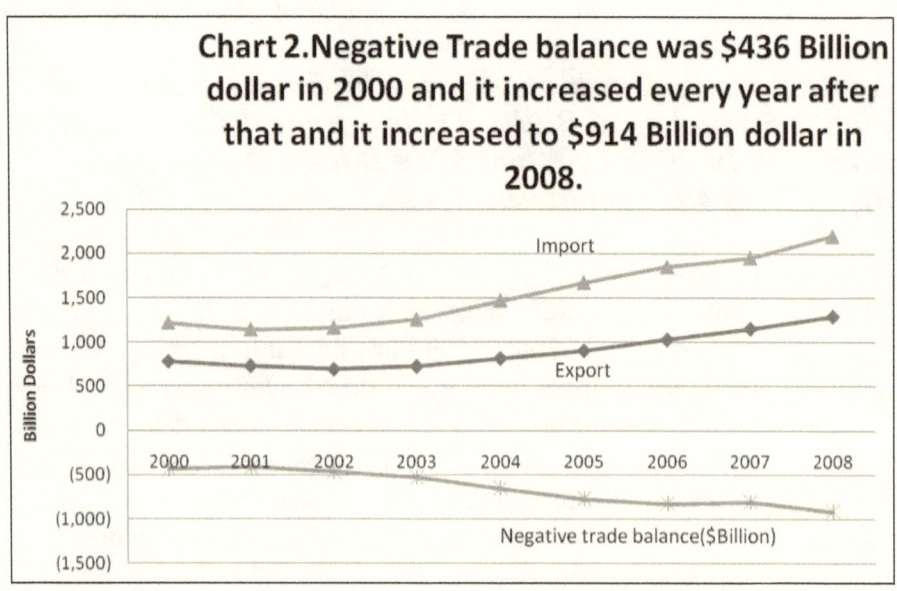

Chart 2. Negative Trade balance was $436 Billion dollar in 2000 and it increased every year after that and it increased to $914 Billion dollar in 2008.

CHAPTER 2:

TEN COUNTRIES WHERE MOST OF THE USA JOBS WERE TRANSFERRED DURING LAST 9 YEARS 2000-2008.

2.1. Highest number of USA jobs was transferred to China during 2000-2008:

In 2008 USA transferred 17.9 million jobs to China, 4.3 million jobs to Mexico, 2.6 million jobs to Canada, 2.5 million jobs to Japan, 2.3 million jobs to Nigeria, 1.4 million jobs to Germany, 0.8 million jobs to Ireland, 0.7 million jobs to Italy.

In 2000 USA transferred 5.6 million jobs to only China which was 26% of total transfer (21.8 million) to all other countries of the world. In 2008 USA transferred 17.9 million jobs to only China which was 39% of total transfer (45.7 million) to all other countries of the world (Table: 3.1).USA transferred 12.3 million more jobs to China in 2008 than 2000. This made USA economy to extremely bad position. Transfer of jobs to China should be reduced to zero or close to zero to create about 17.9 million jobs in USA in a year.

In 2008 USA exported $70 Billion dollars merchandise to China. In 2008 USA imported $338 Billion dollars merchandise from China (Table:3). Import from China should be reduced to $70 Billion dollars to create 17.9 million jobs for USA people.

2.1a. USA trade deficit with China should be reduced to zero or close to zero to create 17.9 million jobs in USA:

USA trade deficit with China was $84 Billon dollars in 2000 (Table: 3). USA trade deficit with China increased to $268 Billion dollar in 2008. 17.9 million jobs can be increased in USA if $268 Billion trade deficit with China be brought down to zero or close to zero.

2.1b. There will not be affect in merchandise price economically if trade deficit with China be reduced to zero or close to zero:

There will be no affect in price in USA economically for that action. Because, USA economy is market economy. USA has sufficient man power to that job. If temporarily 10%-20% price go up, it will come down as more companies will come to that business increasing supply enough to bring down the price.

Products of USA companies will be better in quality and long lasting. If a $1.00 merchandise of other country lasts 1 year and the price of same merchandise of USA companies is $1.20 and lasts 2 years. The economic price of USA produced merchandise is $0.60 cheaper than that made from other country. So, if transfer of 45.7 million job is stopped gradually now, economic price of merchandise will remain same or will go down.

In addition, as the quality of the USA made product will be better, the economic price of USA product merchandise will be cheaper or same although the price of USA made product goes 10%-20% up.

Although 45.7 million jobs were transferred to other countries, price of merchandise had gone up 10%-20% in 2008 due to less sales of merchandise and fixed cost of the companies is same or higher.

As the USA people will have job, they can buy merchandise by 10%-20% higher price.

If a USA family lives on welfare or food stamp, spending $1.00 for a imported cheaper merchandise is hard for them. If that family has $30,000/

year income from job, that family can spend $1.20 for that USA made merchandise easily.

Table 3. Transfer of USA jobs to China from 2000-2008											
Trade			2000	2001	2002	2003	2004	2005	2006	2007	2008
China	Export	($ Billion)	16	19	22	28	35	42	55	65	70
	Import	($ Billion)	100	102	125	152	197	243	288	321	338
	Trade	Balance									
	($ Billion)	(Negative)	(84)	(83)	(103)	(124)	(162)	(201)	(233)	(256)	(268)
	USA jobs	transferred									
	to China (in million)		5.6	5.5	6.9	8.3	10.8	13.4	15.5	17.1	17.9

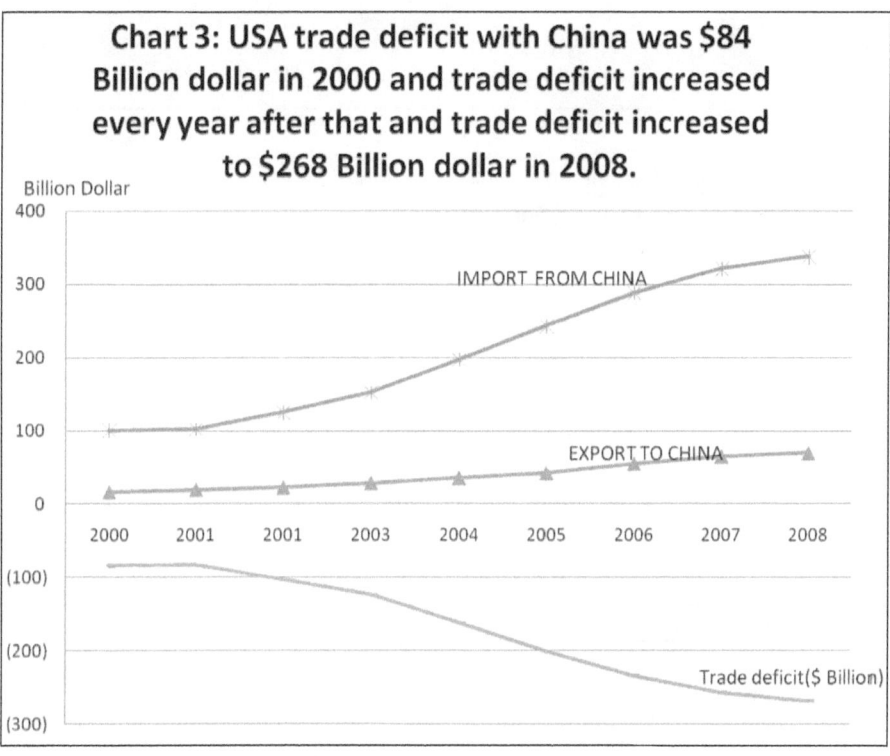

Chart 3: USA trade deficit with China was $84 Billion dollar in 2000 and trade deficit increased every year after that and trade deficit increased to $268 Billion dollar in 2008.

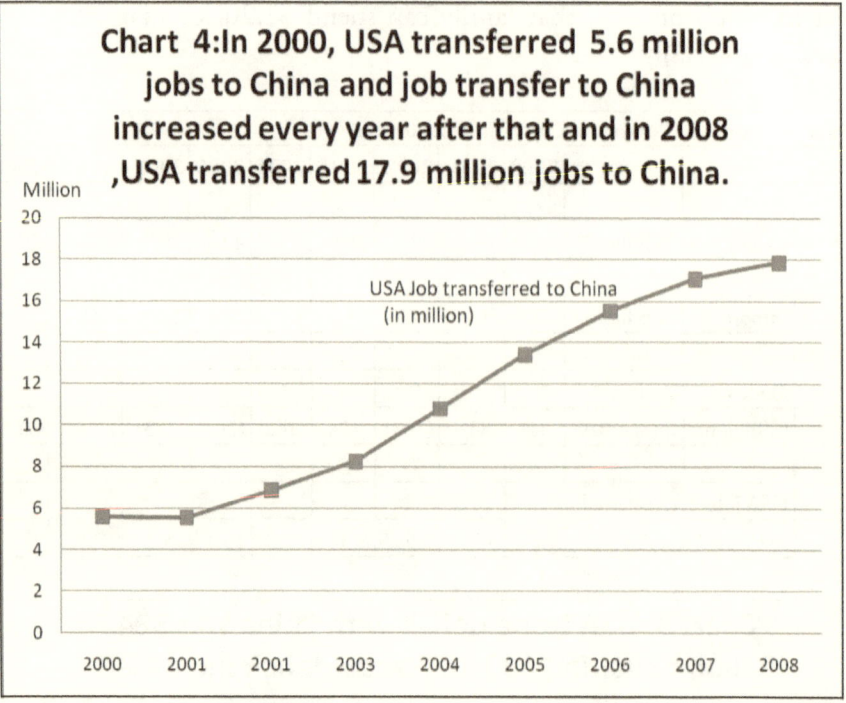

Chart 4:In 2000, USA transferred 5.6 million jobs to China and job transfer to China increased every year after that and in 2008 ,USA transferred 17.9 million jobs to China.

Table 3.1: In 2000, USA transferred China 26% of the total job transfer and job transfer increased every year after that and in 2008 USA transferred China 39% of total job transfer.			
Year	Total job Transfer(Million)	Job transferred to China (Million)	Job transferred to other countries (Million)	% transferred to China only
2000	21.8	5.6	16.2	26
2001	20.6	5.5	15.1	27
2002	23.4	6.9	16.5	29
2003	26.6	8.3	18.3	31
2004	32.8	10.8	22	33

2005	38.6	13.4	25.2	35
2006	41.4	15.5	25.9	37
2007	40.5	17.1	23.4	42
2008	45.7	17.9	27.8	39

2.2. Total USA jobs transferred to Mexico were 1.7 million in 2000 and 4.3 million in 2008:

USA transferred 2.6 million more jobs to Mexico in 2008 than 2000. Transfer of jobs to Mexico should be reduced to zero or close to zero to create about 4.3 million jobs in USA in a year.

In 2008 USA exported $151 Billion dollars merchandise to Mexico. In 2008 USA imported $216 Billion dollars merchandise from Mexico (Table: 4).Import from Mexico should be reduced to $151 Billion dollars to create 4.3 million jobs for USA people. USA trade deficit with Mexico was $25 Billon dollars in 2000 (Table: 3). USA trade deficit with Mexico increased to $65 Billion dollar in 2008. USA trade deficit with Mexico should be reduced to zero or close to zero to create 4.3 million jobs in USA. There will be no affect in price in USA economically for that action. Because, USA economy is market economy.USA has sufficient man power to that job.

	Table 4.Transfer of USA jobs to Mexico from 2000-2008.										
Trade			2000	2001	2002	2003	2004	2005	2006	2007	2008
Mexico	Export	($ Billion)	111	101	97	97	111	120	134	136	151
	Import	($ Billion)	136	131	135	138	156	170	198	211	216
	Trade ($ Billion)	Balance (Negative)	(25)	(30)	(38)	(41)	(45)	(50)	(64)	(75)	(65)
	USA jobs to Mexico (in million)	transferred	1.7	2.0	2.5	2.7	3.0	3.3	4.3	5.0	4.3

2.3. USA trade deficit with Saudi Arabia should be reduced to create job for USA people:

In 2008 USA exported $12 Billion dollars merchandise to Saudi Arabia. In 2008 USA imported $54 Billion dollars merchandise from Saudi Arabia (Table: 5).Import from Saudi Arabia should be reduced to $12 Billion dollars to create jobs for USA people. USA trade deficit with Saudi Arabia was $8 Billon dollars in 2000 (Table: 5). USA trade deficit with Saudi Arabia increased to $42 Billion dollar in 2008. USA trade deficit with Saudi Arabia should be reduced to zero or close to zero to create jobs for USA people. USA should drill oil from it's own land to meet demand for USA people and to stop oil import from other country completely. At the same time USA should develop new substitute to run vehicle instead of oil.

Table 5. USA jobs trade deficit with Saudi Arabia from 2000-2008.											
Trade			2000	2001	2001	2003	2004	2005	2006	2007	2008
Saudi Arabia	Export	($ Billion)	6	6	5	5	5	7	8	10	12
	Import	($ Billion)	14	13	13	18	21	27	32	36	54
	Trade	Balance									
	($ Billion)	(Negative)	(8)	(7)	(8)	(13)	(16)	(20)	(24)	(26)	(42)

2.4. Total USA jobs transferred to Canada were 1.7 million in 2000 and 2.6 million in 2008:

USA transferred 0.9 million more jobs to Canada in 2008 than 2000. Transfer of jobs to Canada should be reduced to zero or close to zero to create about 2.6 million jobs in USA in a year. In 2008 USA exported $261 Billion dollars merchandise to Canada. In 2008 USA imported $339 Billion dollars merchandise from Canada (Table: 6).Import from Canada should be reduced to $261 Billion dollars to create 2.6 million jobs for USA people. USA trade deficit with Canada was $52 Billon dollars in 2000 (Table: 6). USA trade deficit with Canada increased to

$78 Billion dollar in 2008. USA trade deficit with Canada should be reduced to zero or close to zero to create 2.6 million jobs in USA. There will be no affect in price in USA economically for that action. Because, USA economy is free market economy.USA has sufficient manpower to the job.

Trade		Table 6.Transfer of USA jobs to Canada from 2000-2008.									
			2000	2001	2002	2003	2004	2005	2006	2007	2008
Canada	Export	($ Billion)	179	163	161	170	190	212	231	249	261
	Import	($ Billion)	231	216	209	222	256	290	302	317	339
	Trade ($ Billion)	Balance (Negative)	(52)	(53)	(48)	(52)	(66)	(78)	(71)	(68)	(78)
	USA jobs	transferred to Canada (in million)	1.7	1.8	1.6	1.7	2.2	2.6	2.4	2.3	2.6

2.5. USA trade deficit with Venezuela should be reduced to create job for USA people:

In 2008 USA exported $12 Billion dollars merchandise to Venezuela. In 2008 USA imported $51 Billion dollars merchandise from Venezuela (Table: 7).Import from Venezuela should be reduced to $12 Billion dollars to create jobs for USA people. USA trade deficit with Venezuela was $13 Billon dollars in 2000 (Table: 7). USA trade deficit with Venezuela increased to $39 Billion dollar in 2008. USA trade deficit with Venezuela should be reduced to zero or close to zero to create jobs for USA people. USA should drill oil from it's own land to meet demand for USA people and to stop oil import from other country completely. At the same time USA should develop new substitute to run vehicle instead of oil.

Table 7.USA trade deficit with Venezuela from 2000-2008.												
Trade			2000	2001	2002	2003	2004	2005	2006	2007	2008
Venezuela	Export	($ Billions)	6	6	4	3	5	6	9	10	12
	Import	($ Billion)	19	15	15	17	25	34	37	40	51
	Trade ($ Billion)	Balance (Negative)	(13)	(9)	(11)	(14)	(20)	(28)	(28)	(30)	(39)

2.6. Total USA jobs transferred to Japan were 2.7 million in 2000 and 2.5 million in 2008:

Transfer of jobs to Japan should be reduced to zero or close to zero to create about 2.5 million jobs in USA in a year. In 2008 USA exported $65 Billion dollars merchandise to Japan. In 2008 USA imported $139 Billion dollars merchandise from Japan (Table: 8).Import from Japan should be reduced to $65 Billion dollars to create 2.5 million jobs for USA people. USA trade deficit with Japan was $81 Billon dollars in 2000 (Table: 8). USA trade deficit with Japan was $74 Billion dollar in 2008. USA trade deficit with Japan should be reduced to zero or close to zero to create 2.5 million jobs in USA. There will be no affect in price in USA economically for that action. Because, USA economy is free market economy.USA has sufficient man power to that job.

Table 8.Transfer of USA jobs to Japan from 2000-2008.												
Trade			2000	2001	2002	2003	2004	2005	2006	2007	2008
Japan	Export	($ Billion)	65	57	51	52	54	55	60	63	65
	Import	($ Billion)	146	126	121	118	130	138	148	145	139
	Trade ($ Billion)	Balance (Negative)	(81)	(69)	(70)	(66)	(76)	(83)	(88)	(82)	(74)
	USA jobs to Japan (in million)	transferred	2.7	2.3	2.3	2.2	2.5	2.8	2.9	2.7	2.5

2.7. Total USA jobs transferred to Nigeria were 0.7 million in 2000 and 2.3 million in 2008:

Transfer of jobs to Nigeria should be reduced to zero or close to zero to create about 2.3 million jobs in USA in a year(Table:9). Import from Nigeria should be reduced to $4 Billion dollars to create 2.3 million jobs for USA people. USA trade deficit with Nigeria was $10 Billon dollars in 2000 (Table: 9). USA trade deficit with Nigeria was $34 Billion dollar in 2008. USA trade deficit with Nigeria should be reduced to zero or close to zero to create 2.3 million jobs in USA. There will be no affect in price in USA economically for that action. Because, USA economy is market economy.USA has sufficient man power to that job.

Trade			2000	2001	2002	2003	2004	2005	2006	2007	2008
	Table 9.Transfer of USA jobs to Nigeria from 2000-2008.										
Nigeria	Export	($ Billion)	1	1	1	1	2	2	2	3	4
	Import	($ Billion)	11	9	6	10	16	24	28	33	38
	Trade ($ Billion)	Balance (Negative)	(10)	(8)	(5)	(9)	(14)	(22)	(26)	(30)	(34)
	USA jobs to Nigeria (in million)	transferred 0.7	0.5	0.3	0.6	0.9	1.5	1.7	2.0	2.3	

2.8. Total USA jobs transferred to Germany were 1.0 million in 2000 and 1.4 million in 2008:

Transfer of jobs to Germany should be reduced to zero or close to zero to create about 1.4 million jobs in USA in a year. In 2008 USA exported $54 Billion dollars merchandise to Germany. In 2008 USA imported $97 Billion dollars merchandise from Germany (Table: 10).Import from Germany should be reduced to $54 Billion dollars to create 1.4 million jobs for USA people. USA trade deficit with Germany was $30 Billon dollars in 2000(Table: 10). USA trade deficit with Germany increased to $43 Billion dollar in 2008. USA trade deficit with Germany should be reduced to zero or close to zero to create 1.4 million jobs in USA. There will be no affect in price in USA economically for that action. Because, USA economy is free market economy. USA has sufficient man power to that job.

			2000	2001	2002	2003	2004	2005	2006	2007	2008
Table 10. Transfer of USA jobs to Germany from 2000-2008.												
Trade			2000	2001	2002	2003	2004	2005	2006	2007	2008
Germany	Export	($ Billion)	29	30	27	29	31	34	41	50	54
	Import	($ Billion)	59	59	63	68	77	85	89	94	97
	Trade	Balance									
	($ Billion)	(Negative)	(30)	(29)	(36)	(39)	(46)	(51)	(48)	(44)	(43)
	USA jobs	transferred									
	to Germany (in million)		1.0	1.0	1.2	1.3	1.5	1.7	1.6	1.5	1.4

2.9. Total USA jobs transferred to Italy were 0.5 million in 2000 and 0.7 million in 2008:

Transfer of jobs to Italy should be reduced to zero or close to zero to create about 0.7 million jobs in USA in a year. In 2008 USA exported $15 Billion dollars merchandise to Italy. In 2008 USA imported $36 Billion dollars merchandise from Italy (Table: 11). Import from Italy should be reduced to $15 Billion dollars to create 0.7 million jobs for USA people. USA trade deficit with Italy was $14 Billon dollars in 2000 (Table: 11). USA trade deficit with Italy increased to $21 Billion dollar in 2008. USA trade deficit with Germany should be reduced to zero or close to zero to create 0.7 million jobs in USA. There will be no affect in price in USA economically for that action. Because, USA economy is free market economy. USA has sufficient man power to that job.

			2000	2001	2002	2003	2004	2005	2006	2007	2008
Table 11. Transfer of USA jobs to Italy from 2000-2008.												
Trade			2000	2001	2002	2003	2004	2005	2006	2007	2008
	Export	($ Billion)	11	10	10	11	11	12	13	14	15

Italy											
	Import	($ Billion)	25	24	24	25	28	31	33	35	36
	Trade ($ Billion)	Balance (Negative)	(14)	(14)	(14)	(14)	(17)	(19)	(20)	(21)	(21)
	USA jobs to Italy (in million)	transferred	0.5	0.5	0.5	0.5	0.6	0.6	0.7	0.7	0.7

2.10. Total USA jobs transferred to Ireland were 0.3 million in 2000 and 0.8 million in 2008:

Transfer of jobs to Ireland should be reduced to zero or close to zero to create about 0.8 million jobs in USA in a year. In 2008 USA exported $7 Billion dollars merchandise to Ireland. In 2008 USA imported $31 Billion dollars merchandise from Ireland(Table: 12).Import from Ireland should be reduced to $7 Billion dollars to create 0.8 million jobs for USA people. USA trade deficit with Ireland was $8 Billon dollars in 2000 (Table: 12). USA trade deficit with Ireland increased to $24 Billion dollar in 2008. USA trade deficit with Ireland should be reduced to zero or close to zero to create 0.8 million jobs in USA. There will be no affect in price in USA economically for that action. Because, USA economy is market economy. USA has sufficient man power to that job.

Table 12.Transfer of USA jobs to Ireland from 2000-2008.											
Trade			2000	2001	2001	2003	2004	2005	2006	2007	2008
Ireland	Export	($ Billion)	8	7	7	8	8	9	9	9	7
	Import	($ Billion)	16	18	22	26	27	29	29	30	31
	Trade ($ Billion)	Balance (Negative)	(8)	(11)	(15)	(18)	(19)	(20)	(20)	(21)	(24)
	USA jobs to Ireland(in million)	transferred	0.3	0.4	0.5	0.6	0.6	0.7	0.7	0.7	0.8

CHAPTER 3:

USA CAN INCREASE 45.7 MILLION JOBS IN A YEAR STOPPING FULL TRANSFER OF JOBS TO OTHER COUNTRIES.

3.1. USA can increase 45.7 million jobs in a year stopping full transfer of jobs to other countries:

USA can increase 45.7 million jobs by stopping transfer of jobs to other countries(Table:1).By transferring job to other countries USA cannot increase millions of jobs for USA people. This has been proved that there is negative correlation between job transfer and strength of the economy and job. That means, if job transfer increases economy and job goes down and vice versa. There is also negative correlation between trade deficit and strength of the economy and job. That means, if trade deficit increases economy and job goes down and vice versa. The actual data of last 9 years (2000-2008) and the practical situation proved that.

3.2. Now USA economy can go to 2000 level stopping transfer of about 24 million jobs to other countries:

If USA wants to go to 2000 economic strength level now, USA should stop transfer of about 24 million jobs to other countries now. And, 24 million jobs will be created for USA people. Without doing that USA cannot go to 2000 economy strength level.

CHAPTER 4:

USA CAN INCREASE ABOUT 8 MILLION JOBS BY STOPPING JOBS TO UNDOCUMENTED PEOPLE IN USA.

4.1. Undocumented people in USA have occupied about 8 million jobs of documented people:

Undocumented people are working in everywhere in USA. Business man employ undocumented people to pay less than actual salary and to avoid tax. This is very harmful in regards to Government revenue and job crisis. Documented people cannot compete with undocumented as businessman get some monetary advantage. About 8 million jobs can be created in USA if job of undocumented people is stopped for the sake of documented people and Government revenue. Undocumented people is very much harmful for USA economy in 3 main ways:

(a) Undocumented people has taken about 8 million jobs of documented people.
(b) In 2008 USA Government revenue loss was $36.4 billion for transferring 8 million jobs to undocumented people. This will be discussed later of this book.
(c) USA Government can save several Billion dollars expense every year needed to stop flow of undocumented people inside USA.

CHAPTER 5:

TAX REVENUE LOSS OF USA GOVERNMENT WAS $71.2 BILLION DOLLARS FOR TRANSFERRING 45.7 MIILION JOBS TO OTHER COUNTRIES IN 2008.

5.1. USA Government lost $71.2 Billion dollar tax revenue in 2008 for transferring 45.7 million jobs to other countries:

In 2008 USA Government lost $71.8 Billion dollars tax revenue by transferring 45.7 million jobs to other countries(Table:13).

Table 13.USA Government lost $71.2 Billion dollars tax revenue in 2008 for transferring 45.7 million jobs to other countries in 2008.				
Job transferred in 2008(Million)	Tax/Week/Labor	Tax/Year/Labor	US Govt lost Tax Revenue in 2008 ($Billion).	
45.7	$30*	$1,560	$71.2	
*Considering average $30 total tax per week per labor.				

CHAPTER 6:

USA GOVERNMENT COULD SAVE $136.8 BILLION DOLLAR FOODSTAMP AND WELFARE MONEY IN 2008 STOPPING 45.7 MILLION JOB TRANSFER TO OTHER COUNTRIES.

6.1. USA Government could save $136.8 Billion dollar in 2008 stopping 45.7 million job transfer to other countries:

USA Government could save $136.8 Billion dollars Food stamp and Welfare money in 2008 stopping transfer of 45.7 million jobs to other countries in 2008(Table:14).

Table14: Money USA Government could save $136.8 Billion dollars food stamp and welfare money in 2008 stopping 45.7 million jobs transfer to other countries in 2008.			
Job transferred in 2008(Million)	Family suffered in 2008(Million)	Foodstamp & Welfare/Family	Govt Cost could be saved in 2008 ($ Billion)
45.7	22.8	$500*	$136.8
* Considering $500/Family/Month food stamp and/or welfare.			

CHAPTER 7:

TOTAL US GOVERNMENT REVENUE LOSS WAS $208 BILLION DOLLARS IN 2008 FOR TRANSFERRING 45.7 MILLION JOBS TO OTHER COUNTRIES.

7.1. USA Government lost $208 billion dollar revenue in 2008 for transferring 45.7 million jobs to other countries:

USA Government lost $208 billion dollar revenue in 2008 for transferring 45.7 million jobs to other countries(Table 15).USA government could save $136.8 Billion dollars Food stamp and Welfare cost in 2008 and could increase $71.2 tax revenue in 2008 by stopping 45.7 million jobs to other countries in 2008.

Table 15:Total USA Government revenue loss in 2008 was $208 Billion Dollars for transferring 45.7 million jobs to other countries in 2008.

US Govt could save food stamp and Welfare in 2008($Billion)	US Govt loss of tax revenue in 2008($Billion)	Total Revenue loss($Billion)
$136.8	$71.2	$208.0

CHAPTER 8:

US GOVERNMENT LOST $12.4 BILLION DOLLAR TAX REVENUE IN 2008 FOR NOT STOPPING JOBS TO UNDOCUMENTED PEOPLE.

8.1. US Government lost $12.4 Billion dollar tax revenue in 2008 for not stopping Jobs to undocumented people:

US Government lost $12.4 Billion dollar tax revenue in 2008 for not stopping Jobs to undocumented people(Table:16).

Table 16: US Government lost $12.8 Billion dollars tax revenue in 2008 for not stopping 8 million jobs to undocumented people in 2008.			
Job transferred in 2008(Million)	Tax/Week/Labor	Tax/Year/Labor	US Govt lost Tax Revenue in 2008 ($Billion).
8	$30*	$1,560	$12.4
*Considering $30 total tax per week per labor.			

CHAPTER 9:

US GOVERNMENT COULD SAVE $24 BILLION DOLLAR FOODSTAMP AND WELFARE MONEY IN 2008 IF 8 MILLION JOBS TO UNCOCUMENTED PEOPLE COULD BE STOPPED.

9.1. US Government could save $24 Billion dollar food stamp and welfare money in 2008 stopping 8 million jobs of undocumented people:

US Government could save $24 Billion dollar food stamp and welfare money in 2008 stopping 8 million jobs of undocumented people(Table: 17).

Table17: USA Government can save $24 Billion dollars in food stamp and welfare by stopping 8 million jobs to undocumented people in 2008.			
Job transferred to undocumented in 2008(Million)	Family suffered in 2008(Million)	Foodstamp & Welfare/Family	Govt Cost can be saved in 2008 ($Billion)
8	4	$500*	$24.00
* Considering $500/Family/Month food stamp and welfare.			

CHAPTER 10:

TOTAL USA GOVERNMENT REVENUE LOSS WAS $36.4 BILLION DOLLAR IN 2008 FOR NOT STOPPING 8 MILLION JOBS OF UNDOCUMENTED PEOPLE.

10.1. Total USA Government revenue loss was $36.4 Billion dollar in 2008 for not stopping 8 million jobs of undocumented people:

Total USA Government revenue loss was $36.4 Billion dollar in 2008 for not stopping 8 million jobs of undocumented people (Table:18).

Table 18: Total USA Government revenue loss $36.4 Billion dollars in 2008 for not stopping 8 million jobs to undocumented people in 2008.		
US Govt could save money for food stamp & Welfare in 2008($Billion)	US Govt loss of tax revenue in 2008($Billion)	Total Revenue loss($Billion)
$24.00	$12.4	$36.4

10.2 If undocumented people do not get job, USA Government can save Billions Dollar expense needed for border security and immigration:

USA Government spent Billions dollars to stop entrance of undocumented people in USA in each year. If undocumented people do not get job in USA, undocumented will not try to come to USA. Thus, USA Government could save Billions dollars Government revenue which was spent before to stop their entrance and immigration.

CHAPTER 11:

$914 BILLION DOLLAR PURCHASING POWER OF USA PEOPLEWILL INCREASE IF TRANSFER OF USA JOBS TO OTHER COUNTRIES FULLYSTOPPED.

11.1. $914 Billion dollar purchasing power of USA people will increase if 45.7 million Job transfer to other countries is stopped:

If USA Government can stop 45.7 million job transfer to other countries, purchasing power of USA people will increase by $914 Billion dollars(Table:19).

USA companies will not go out of business for lack of sale. Income of USA companies will increase.

Table 19. Serious reduction of purchasing power($Billion) of people of USA for transferring 45.7 million jobs to other countries in 2008.										
		2000	2001	2002	2003	2004	2005	2006	2007	2008
Reduction of										
Purchasing power		(436)	(412)	(468)	(532)	(655)	(772)	(828)	(809)	(914)
($ Billion)										

11.2. USA Government revenue will increase by Billions dollars for sale tax and income tax:

As purchasing power of USA people will increase by several hundred Billion dollars, USA Government revenue from sale tax and income tax will increase by Billions of Dollar.

CHAPTER 12:

THERE WILL BE NO AFFECT IN MERCHANDISE PRICE ECONOMICALLY IF TRANSFER OF 45.7 MILLION JOBS TO OTHER COUNTRIES ARE STOPPED FULLY OR PARTIALLY.

12.1. If transfer of 24 million jobs is stopped, the US economy will go to 2000 strength level and there will not be affect in merchandise price economically:

There will be no affect in merchandise price economically as USA has market economy and USA has sufficient man power to do that job. If temporarily 10%-20% price go up, it will come down as more companies will come to that business increasing supply enough to bring down the price.

Products of USA companies will be better in quality and long lasting. If a $1.00 merchandise of other country lasts 1 year and the price of same merchandise of USA companies is $1.20 and lasts 2 years. The economic price of USA produced merchandise is $0.60 cheaper than that made from other country. So, if transfer of 24 million job is stopped gradually now, economic price of merchandise will remain same or will go down.

In addition, as the quality of the USA made product will be better, the economic price of USA product merchandise will be cheaper or same although the price of USA made product goes 10%-20% up.

Although 45.7 million jobs were transferred to other countries, price of merchandise had gone up 10%-20% in 2008 due to less sales of merchandise and fixed cost of the companies is same or higher.

As the USA people will have job, they can buy merchandise by 10%-20% higher price.

If a USA family lives on welfare or food stamp, spending $1.00 for a imported cheaper merchandise is hard for them. If that family has $30,000/year income from job, that family can spend $1.20 for that USA product merchandise easily.

12.2. If transfer of 45.7 million jobs is stopped, the US economy will go to better level than 2000 and there will be no affect in merchandise price economically:

If transfer of 45.7 million jobs is stopped, the US economy will go to better level than 2000 and there will be no affect in merchandise price economically for the same reasons describe above.

CHAPTER 13:

PRESENT ECONOMIC RECESSION OF USA WAS CREATED BY USA GOVERNMENT BY TRANSFERRING JOBS OF USA PEOPLE TO PEOPLE OF OTHER COUNTRIES.

13.1. Present economic recession was created by USA government policy:

Present economic recession was not occurred automatically rather it was created by USA Government policy.

Transferring 45.7 million jobs to other countries, USA has fallen down to the hole of economic recession. Because, this USA Government policy has reduced $914 Billion dollars purchasing power USA people. As purchasing power of USA people seriously reduced, USA companies could not sale their merchandise and has gone out of business.

CHAPTER 14:

SOCIAL EFFECT OF STOPPING TRANSFER OF USA JOB TO OTHER COUNTRIES.

14.1.If all USA people get jobs, crime will be reduced and spending to stop crime could be reduced effectively:

If all USA people get jobs, crime will be reduced and spending to stop crime could be reduced effectively. USA Government could save Billions dollars and Government revenue will increase by Billion dollars.

14.2. If crime is reduced, the people of USA can live peacefully with pleasure:

If crime is reduced, the people can live peacefully with pleasure. This is also a great social achievement after stopping the transfer of USA jobs to other countries.

CHAPTER 15:

IF REVENUE OF USA GOVERNMENT INCREASES, USA CAN INCREASE HELP TO PEOPLE OF OTHER COUTRIES FOR ECONOMIC DEVELOPMENT AND NATURAL DISASTER EFFECTIVELY.

15.1. If revenue of USA increases every year, USA can increase help to people of other countries for economic development:

If USA Government stop transfer of 45.7 million jobs to other countries, USA Government revenue will increase about $500 Billion dollars a year. USA Government can spend about half of that money every year for economic development of developing countries of the world by opening USA AID offices to developing countries of the world. USA Government will use that money for construction of bridges roads and highways, rehabilitation of poor and homeless people, food aid to poor and homeless people, self sufficiency project of poor and homeless people, controlling major diseases, improvement of agriculture and industry, increase of jobs for all types of people, and housing for poor and homeless people, and other economic development aspects.

15.2. If revenue of USA increases every year, USA can increase help to people of other countries for natural disaster:

If any natural disaster occurs in any country, the country expects bigger USA help generally. If USA stopped transfer of USA jobs to other countries, USA Government revenue will increase enough and USA Government can stand by the side of the country with sufficient resources for necessary time for economic development.

CHAPTER 16:

ONE TRILLION DOLLAR ECONOMIC STIMULUS PLAN CAN NOT INCREASE EMPLOYMENT TO 2000 LEVEL

16.1. One trillion dollar economic stimulus plan cannot increase employment to 2000 level:

USA job transfer to other countries increased 23.9 millions from 2000 to 2008. If one trillion dollar stimulus plan can increase 4 million job in USA, still there will be necessary to increase 19.9 million jobs in other ways to bring employment to 2000 level (Table:19).

Table 20.One trillion dollar economic stimulus plan cannot increase employment to 2000 level.								
	2008*							
Job Transfer increased								
from 2000-2008(in Million)	23.9							
Trillion dollar stimulus								
if can increase job	4.0							
(in million).								
Job Shortage at 2000	19.9							
level(in Million)								
*21.8 million jobs were transferred in 2000 and 45.7 million jobs were transferred in 2008.								

CHAPTER 17:

IF A COUNTRY HAS UNEMPLOYMENT PROBLEM, THAT COUNTRY SHOULD NOT IMPORT THOSE MERCHANDISE WHICH THE PEOPLE OF THAT COUNTRY CAN MAKE.

17.1: If a country has unemployment problem, the country should not import those merchandise from other countries which the people of the country can make:

If a country does not follow that unemployment will increase every year. The economy of the country will go downward.

CHAPTER 18:

RECOMMENDATION

1. USA Government should stop transfer of 45.7 million jobs to other countries now to create 45.7 million jobs for USA people in a year. If USA Government do that, $208 Billion dollars Government revenue will increase in a year

2. USA Government should stop the job of undocumented people inside USA. If USA Government do that, about 8 million new jobs will be created for documented people and $36.4 Billion dollars Government revenue will increase in a year.

3. Present economic recession was created by wrong economic policy of USA Government. Economic recession will be over within a few months permanently and will never come back if economic policy described in this book is adopted.

4. If a country has unemployment problem, the country should not import those merchandise from other countries which people of the country can make.

5. There was negative correlation between job transfer and strength of economy. If USA job transfer to other countries increases, USA economy goes down and vice versa.

6. There was negative correlation between trade deficit and employment/strength of economy. If USA trade deficit with other countries increases, employment/strength of economy goes down and vice versa.

7. USA should reduce transfer of jobs to China to zero or close zero to increase 17.9 million jobs for USA people in a year. Import from China should be reduced to $70 Billion dollar to increase 17.9 million jobs for USA people.

8. There will not be any affect in merchandise price economically in USA if import from China is reduced to $70 Billion /year to create 17.9 million jobs for USA people.

9. USA should reduce transfer of jobs to Mexico to zero or close zero to increase 4.3 million jobs for USA people in a year. Import from Mexico should be reduced to $151 Billion dollar to increase 4.3 million jobs for USA people.

10. USA should reduce transfer of jobs to Canada to zero or close zero to increase 2.6 million jobs for USA people in a year. Import from Canada should be reduced to $261 Billion dollar to increase 2.6 million jobs for USA people.

11. USA should reduce transfer of jobs to Japan to zero or close zero to increase 2.5 million jobs for USA people in a year. Import from Japan should be reduced to $65 Billion dollar to increase 2.5 million jobs for USA people.

12. USA should reduce transfer of jobs to Nigeria to zero or close zero to increase 2.3 million jobs for USA people in a year. Import from Nigeria should be reduced to $4 Billion dollar to increase 2.3 million jobs for USA people.

13. USA should reduce transfer of jobs to Germany to zero or close zero to increase 1.4 million jobs for USA people in a year. Import from Germany should be reduced to $54 Billion dollar to increase 1.4 million jobs for USA people.

14. USA should reduce transfer of jobs to Italy to zero or close zero to increase 0.7 million jobs for USA people in a year. Import from Italy should be reduced to $15 Billion dollar to increase 0.7 million jobs for USA people.

15. USA should reduce transfer of jobs to Ireland to zero or close zero to increase 0.8 million jobs for USA people in a year. Import from Ireland should be reduced to $7 Billion dollar to increase 0.8 million jobs for USA people.

16. USA should dig their own oil from own territory to lift oil to reduce $42 Billion dollar trade deficit with Saudi Arabia and $39 Billion dollar trade deficit with Venezuela. This will create jobs for USA people and Government revenue will increase $81 Billion dollar in a year. At the same time, USA should develop technology to reduce oil dependency for better environment.

17. $914 Billion dollar purchasing power of USA people will increase in a year and no business or company will close down for lack of

sale. Rather Billions dollar Government revenue will increase from sale tax and income tax.

18. USA should increase 23.9 million jobs to bring the economy to 2000 strength level. Economic policy described in this book could increase 45.7 million jobs in a year.

19. Now USA has trillion dollar deficit budget. Economic policy described in this book can give balanced budget for USA after one year. After that USA can make surplus budget.

20. If revenue of USA Government increases, USA can increase help to people of other countries for economic development and natural disaster effectively.

21. This book can help to other countries to increase job and Government revenue.

REFERENCES

1. US Statistical Abstract, 2009. U S Department of Commerce, USA.

www.ingramcontent.com/pod-product-compliance
Lightning Source LLC
Chambersburg PA
CBHW021926170526
45157CB00005B/2204